General editor: Graham Hand

Brodie's Notes on George Bernard Shaw's

Arms and the Man

Norman T. Carrington MA

M

MACMILLAN

First published by James Brodie Ltd
Revised edition published 1976 by Pan Books Ltd

This revised edition published 1993 by
THE MACMILLAN PRESS LTD
Houndmills, Basingstoke, Hampshire RG21 2XS
and London
Companies and representatives
throughout the world

ISBN 0–333–58195–4

Typeset by Footnote Graphics, Warminster, Wiltshire
Printed in Great Britain by
Cox & Wyman Ltd, Reading

Contents

Preface by the general editor 5

The author and his work 7

The play 24
Title 24
Plot 24

**Act summaries, critical commentary, textual notes
and revision questions 26**

The characters 40
Raina 41
Sergius 44
Bluntschli 46
Minor characters 48

Theme 52

Style 55

General questions and sample answer in note form 59

Further reading 61

Preface

The intention throughout this study aid is to stimulate and guide, to encourage your involvement in the book, and to develop informed responses and a sure understanding of the main details.

Brodie's Notes provide a clear outline of the play or novel's plot, followed by act, scene, or chapter summaries and/or commentaries. These are designed to emphasize the most important literary and factual details. Poems, stories or non-fiction texts combine brief summary with critical commentary on individual aspects or common features of the genre being examined. Textual notes define what is difficult or obscure and emphasize literary qualities. Revision questions are set at appropriate points to test your ability to appreciate the prescribed book and to write accurately and relevantly about it.

In addition, each of these Notes includes a critical appreciation of the author's art. This covers such major elements as characterization, style, structure, setting and themes. Poems are examined technically – rhyme, rhythm, for instance. In fact, any important aspect of the prescribed work will be evaluated. The aim is to send you back to the text you are studying.

Each study aid concludes with a series of general questions which require a detailed knowledge of the book: some of these questions may invite comparison with other books, some will be suitable for coursework exercises, and some could be adapted to work you are doing on another book or books. Each study aid has been adapted to meet the needs of the current examination requirements. They provide a basic, individual and imaginative response to the work being studied, and it is hoped that they will stimulate you to acquire disciplined reading habits and critical fluency.

Graham Handley 1990

A close reading of the play is the student's primary task. These Notes will help to increase your understanding and appreciation of the play, and to stimulate *your own* thinking about it; *they are in no way intended as a substitute* for a thorough knowledge of the book.

These notes can be used with any edition of the play.

I lay my eternal curse on whomsoever shall now or at any time hereafter make schoolbooks of my works, and make me hated, as Shakespear is hated. My plays were not designed as instruments of torture.

Bernard Shaw, in a letter dated 24th November, 1927.

The author and his work

George Bernard Shaw, the most provocative controversialist of the first half of the twentieth century, was born in Dublin on 26th July, 1856, in a very ordinary home. It was a poor home and it was an unhappy home. His father made an indifferent sort of living as a corn broker, but the family made ends meet by taking in a teacher of singing, called Lee, as a paying guest. Lee discovered that Shaw's mother had a beautiful mezzo-soprano voice and he trained it. But when after some years he sought his fortune in London, the Shaw family were left with a house they could not afford on their hands. Mrs. Shaw gave up the unequal struggle and, following Lee's example, set off for London with her two daughters (both older than Bernard) in 1871, and there established herself as a teacher of singing and music, leaving her fifteen-year-old son and his father to go into lodgings.

The boy had had lessons from an uncle who was a clergyman and eventually had entered the Wesleyan Connexional School, Dublin (now Wesley College). His entry in *Who's Who* in his lifetime read, 'Educated at Wesley College, Dublin, *and other boy prisons*'. From all accounts he was none too satisfactory a pupil, but this should not be taken too seriously, as great men always have a tendency to belittle their education and Shaw was never afraid of advertising what he owed to his own unaided efforts. But whatever he owed to his schooling certain it is that he owed infinitely more to the appreciation of music and painting given him at home by his mother, and to his own love of reading. He read anything and everything that came his way, not only regular children's classics like *The Arabian Nights*, *The Pilgrim's Progress* and *Robinson Crusoe*, but *The Faerie Queene*, the poems of Byron and most of the novels of Scott and Dickens.

At fifteen years of age he was apprenticed to a Dublin land agent. His ability was obvious from the first and a year later he became the firm's cashier, replacing a man of forty! But the thought of spending his life at an office desk weighed him down. As the years wore on he could not stand it, and in 1876 he left and joined his mother in London.

'All rising to great place,' says Bacon, 'is by a winding stair.' It was not an easy time for a man to launch out on a new career. In that year a slump hit the country such as it was not to see again until 1931, and people did not have the money for books and magazines. Nine years he spent in hack-writing and odd jobs for business firms, and during this time, he tells us, he made no more than £5 9s. 6d. by his pen. But, in between times, to quote his own words, 'I made a man of myself (at my mother's expense) instead of a slave'. In other words he wrote five novels, for none of which he could find a publisher, his explanation being that his style was a hundred and fifty years behind the times and his ideas a hundred and fifty years ahead of them! He even sent the manuscripts of his novels to New York publishers, but with no better sequel. Blackwood's did accept one of them, but withdrew their acceptance within a few weeks. It was nearly fifty years before his first novel, *Immaturity*, was published. It was justly named. When he had made a name for himself as a playwright, of course, publishers were clamouring for anything he could give them – they were sure of a sale simply because a book bore his name. The other four novels were *Cashel Byron's Profession* (generally reckoned to be the best), *The Irrational Knot, The Unsocial Socialist* and *Love Among the Artists*. They were all written in business-like fashion – so many pages a day, come wet or fine. But Shaw would not have it that he ever had to 'struggle' for a living. Looking back on his career, 'I never struggled,' he declared, 'I rose by sheer gravitation.'

Be that as it may, it was not until he turned to criticism that Shaw made any headway. He became acquainted with William Archer, one of the reviewers of *The Pall Mall Gazette*, and at one time when he was hard-pressed Archer gave Shaw a book to review. This review set him off on his career, and after that he had as much book reviewing for *The Pall Mall Gazette* as he cared to do, at two guineas per thousand words. He made £112 in his first year as a critic. Archer was also theatre critic for *The World*, and just at this time the art critic of *The World* died and Archer was asked to take on the job. Archer knew nothing about pictures, but Shaw did, so Archer recommended him, and he became art critic to *The World* at fivepence a line. In 1885 he became music critic of *The Star*, under the cumbrous pseudonym of Corno di Bassetto (the name of an obsolete musical instrument) at two guineas a week. He was now finding the practical value of the judgement of painting and music which he had early assimilated from his mother. After two years Corno di Bassetto became music critic to *The World* also, making £5 a week from contributions to the two papers. The word 'brilliant' was now being freely applied to his work. Before very long he felt sure enough of himself to discard his pseudonym and sign his articles G.B.S. Not only was his work well-spoken of, but he was business-like, and one thing that won him commendation from editors was that he was always on time with his work. In the early nineties he became dramatic critic of *The Saturday Review*, and in addition to his regular weekly articles from time to time he contributed other reviews of books and pictures for the papers with which he was associated. His money troubles were now at an end.

But it was his spare-time activities that gave zest to his life rather than the daily round and common task. He studied Karl Marx and made himself prominent in the early Socialist movement, and in 1884 became one of the founders of the Fabian Society. All his life he called himself a Socialist, but at this time he 'worked at it' – writing innumerable Fabian tracts and speaking on Fabian platforms (sometimes two or three times a day). Two of his early plays, *Widowers' Houses* and *Mrs. Warren's Profession*, have a Socialist flavour, but since then his Socialist view-point has been kept out of his plays. Much later, in 1928, he gave his political creed a volume to itself in *The Intelligent Woman's Guide to Socialism and Capitalism*. But, as in everything else, Shaw is essentially individual, and his beliefs cannot be identified with those of any one political party, and in their hey-day he expressed admiration for Lenin, Mussolini and Hitler with equal fervour. But in the eighties and nineties of the last century he closely identified himself with the growing Socialist movement and grudged every minute he was not working for it. Since then he has become something of a capitalist by telling the world unpleasant truths about itself that it does not want to know but has been eager to buy. One of his fads at this time was living on greens and water, and the result of continual hard work on a diet like this was that in 1898 he had a complete breakdown. His recovery was due to the attentions of the 'heroic lady' whom he married when he was better, Charlotte Frances Payne-Townshend. After this he engaged less actively in political propaganda and in a few years gave it up altogether.

Shaw is the only modern dramatist who started to write plays which were *read* and not *acted*. For nearly two years most of his plays were published but not acted. It would appear that he thought of his plays as being read and not seen, at all events at the beginning of the fourth paragraph of the Epilogue to *Androcles and the Lion* he writes, 'All my articulate Christians, the *reader* will notice, have different enthusiasms'. The extended stage directions give the same impression. All his plays are problem plays and were intended to be read in conjunction with a preface. It was 1904 before his plays were produced regularly. True, *Widowers' Houses*, his first, was produced at the Royalty Theatre in 1892, but it was no great success and was soon forgotten until after the first world-war it made a hit in Berlin. Socialists in England welcomed it as propaganda, but in those early days Socialism was regarded as the creed of a few extremists and the general public turned a cold shoulder. That, of course, is the reason why it was written. Shaw intended to use the theatre for propaganda. He declared that the man who believed in art for art's sake is a fool, a hopeless fool, and in a state of 'damnation'. Art is too great to be comprehended in a formal doctrine such as 'art for art's sake'; none the less one would think Shaw too great a man to dismiss such a doctrine with a contemptuous wave of the hand. If the author lets his meaning overpower him or interrupt him, he will be no great artist. The life and spirit of art, that glorious thing in us which makes us feel the beautiful, the true and the good, is not propaganda, but maybe it is the spirit which prompts that propaganda. We wrong a play when we compel it to argue. A play must have some purpose, or it is lawless, but the purpose must not interfere; the play must be *an expression* of the purpose and not an excuse for conveying it; a vehicle not a cloak; part and parcel of it, not patched on. The moral that lies in a thing is very different from the moral that is dragged out of it. The purpose of art is rather 'art for *life's* sake'. *Widowers' Houses* is an attack on the slum evil in our cities. Trench is the type who is an idealist only so long as his idealism does not empty his pocket, and like Dickens and Thackeray and Galsworthy, Shaw sees through the snobbery and hyprocrisy of social life, and he unveils it more ruthlessly than any. Even *Pygmalion*, which no one would think of interpreting as propaganda had he not read the *Preface*, is, Shaw says, 'intensely and deliberately didactic'.

Arms and The Man, Shaw's second play, was the first to be performed in a regular West End theatre, the Avenue Theatre in Northumberland Avenue, in 1894. This was owing to the generosity of a Miss Horniman, daughter of a wealthy tea merchant. Shaw wrote the play for Miss Florence Farr, who had joined the management of the Avenue Theatre (it was she who took the part of Louka). She asked Shaw to let her revive *Widowers' Houses*, but he preferred a new play to the revival of an old one, and *Arms and The Man* was 'hastily completed', as Shaw says in the Preface. It ran for eleven weeks, but only to half-full houses, and financially was a disastrous failure. It cost £4,000 and the total receipts were no more than £1,777! Yet in the Preface to *Plays Pleasant* (1898) Shaw boasts that 'It passed for a success'. It would certainly be true to say this today, however, when it has been produced all over the world. In the play Shaw tilts at romance — romance in warfare. Romance is false. Shaw must see life as it is, without qualification, compromise or sparing anyone's feelings. He always calls a spade a spade. In *Man and Superman* the idea that woman is the pursued and man the pursuer, the conventional belief, is shown to hide the reality. *How he Lied to*

Her Husband is another tilt at romance. Romantic convention assumes that husbands are jealous admirers of their wives. Mr. Bompas, her husband, gets angry only when Henry, his wife's lover, pretends he has no love for her. Things are turned inside out again, our conventional ideas are swept away by the author's delightful wit and paradox. Whatever the faith of the public Shaw is certain to enjoy pulling it to pieces. People take it for granted that man has progressed immeasurably since the days of Caesar and Cleopatra, and that those were cruel times. In *Androcles and the Lion* and *Caesar and Cleopatra*, Shaw makes us realise that in those days people in authority acted and their subjects reacted to things in exactly the same was as they do now. The public believes implicitly what it is told by doctors. Shaw must unmask them in *The Doctor's Dilemma*. The public believes that Joan of Arc was a saint, grossly wronged by the wicked men of her day and generation, but in *Saint Joan* he shows that if she appeared on earth today people would look at her in exactly the same light as our ancestors did five centuries ago. One of Shaw's ideas seems to be that human nature cannot be changed: Ferrovius cannot forbear slaying the gladiators, although full of an inward resolve to follow Christ his master; Cleopatra is a savage still, after all Caesar's efforts to improve her; men would still reject Joan of Arc in the twentieth century, if she came back to us.

Between 1892 and 1940 Shaw wrote no fewer than fifty plays (roughly one a year), and at least until he was seventy there was no decline either in his mental energy or his creative impulse. 'A perpetual holiday is a good working definition of hell', he once said. The best work of most authors has been produced in the prime of life. *Saint Joan*, reckoned by most people to be his masterpiece, was written when he was nearly seventy. It strikes every chord from happy laughter to poignant tragedy. It had an immense success in New York, at Christmas 1923, and again in London in 1924, with Sybil Thorndike in the title part. Revivals of it have been frequent, generally running for several weeks. It was no doubt owing to the impression made by *Saint Joan* that Shaw was awarded the Nobel Prize for Literature in 1926 (six years before Galsworthy). In Shaw's earlier plays the theme generally has a slant towards economic affairs, but in the later plays the emphasis is a religious one. Edmund Wilson says that Shaw's plays 'have been a truthful and continually developing chronicle of a soul in relation to society'. In that case the change is significant. *Androcles and the Lion* and *Saint Joan*, Shaw's greatest play, bring religious views into prominence. To state Shaw's constant beliefs on *anything* is difficult, most of all his religious beliefs: he liked to pose as an enigma and consequently whatever statement is made about his beliefs can be contradicted somewhere in his work. 'I say that Life Force is God,' wrote Shaw, and perhaps St. John Ervine's summary of his religious outlook is the best.

God, or the Life Force, is an imperfect power striving to become perfect . . . The whole of time has been occupied by God in experiments with instruments invented to help Him in His attempt to perfect Himself. God created a new instrument, Man, who is still on probation. Shaw warns the world that if we, too, fail to achieve God's purpose He will become impatient and scrap mankind as He scrapped the mammoth beasts.

In the main Shaw's plays have been kept alive in England by Repertory Companies and stage societies, though there have been long runs with star actors. His friend Barry Jackson, the proprietor of the Birmingham Repertory Theatre, in association with John Drinkwater (the author of *Abraham Lincoln*) did as much to 'bring out' Shaw as anyone. He made a success of *Heartbreak House* (which Shaw called his best play) at the Birmingham 'Rep.' and, to everyone's amazement, of the long play *Back to Methuselah*, which took five nights to perform. *Pygmalion* was Shaw's first theatrical success in a large commercial theatre (though *Fanny's First Play* had had a long and successful run at a Repertory Theatre – the Little Theatre in the Adelphi, 1911). *Arms and The Man* was the first Shaw play to be produced in New York (17th September, 1894) and since 1910 his plays have been produced regularly in U.S.A., though he has never been a tremendous hit there (*i.e.* as a dramatist – *My Fair Lady* is not Shaw). He swore he would never set foot in U.S.A., but he did make a brief visit on his world tour in 1938 – he 'did' U.S.A., as the Americans themselves would say.

In 1929 Sir Barry Jackson arranged a festival of Shaw's plays at Malvern, inaugurated by a new play, *The Apple Cart*. Shaw was in his element at the festival, walking about the town wearing odd clothes, doing odd things and uttering the most queer opinions, facing the camera as often as he could and generally enjoying a public adulation second only to that given to film stars. 'Malvern', said J. B. Priestley, 'was full of Shaw'. But he was living on his reputation – *The Apple Cart* was feeble by the side of *Saint Joan*. At best it is second-rate Shaw. Sir Barry Jackson continued the festival the following year, but it was not an all-Shavian programme, and in 1931 there was no Shaw play at all. The festival of plays at Malvern was recently revived, but it soon ran into financial difficulties and was not continued.

For some reason Shaw showed intense opposition to having his plays filmed, and for a long time withstood all entreaties and bribes. Eventually, however, he gave way, but, since he insisted that the dialogue of the film *Arms and The Man* should follow that of the play, it turned out a failure. Shaw's great weakness was an excessive dogmatism. He thought he knew everything that there was to know about everything and well earned the reputation of being 'difficult'. He was aware of this, as he says in the Preface (p. 14/*10*), 'I half suspect that those managers who have had most to do with me, if asked to name the main obstacle to the performance of my plays, would unhesitatingly and unanimously reply "The author"'. In 1938 *Pygmalion*, his most characteristic but not his greatest play, was filmed. Shaw always liked to have a hand in the first production of his plays in London, and, characteristically enough, after having refused to allow a film to be made, when it was made he himself supervised its production and wrote most of the script. The film won the Oscar award. For a long time it was not generally known that about 1912 Shaw acted as a cowboy in a film for Barrie. After having a good time at a dinner party of literary men on the invitation of Mr. Asquith, at the Savoy Hotel, Shaw, Chesterton, Barrie and one or two others went down to Elstree and rigged themselves up as cowboys. Then they did all sorts of insane things – chased horses, rode motor-cycles and crawled in and out of drain pipes. In one scene Shaw had to ride over a 'precipice' with five people behind him on a motor-cycle. Unfortunately, however, Barrie scrapped the film. Whatever its success might have been as a film it would certainly have been interesting as a commentary on the leisure-time activities of literary men! A photograph of the group may be seen in Shaw's house.

The film of *Pygmalion* followed Sir Beerbohm Tree's first stage production of the play in England. As a result of its success negotiations were in progress for filming others of Shaw's plays when the war caused the project to be shelved, but since the war *Caesar and Cleopatra*, *Saint Joan* and *The Devil's Disciple* have appeared as films, and, as a whole, they were truer to the play original than *Pygmalion*.

In 1956 a sentimental, romantic, musical version of *Pygmalion*, called *My Fair Lady*, became the rage of New York and set up a Broadway record-breaking run of over six years (2621 performances), getting Shaw's wit and purpose across at popular level. In London it ran for over four years at the Theatre Royal, Drury Lane, the second-longest London run, and subsequently a film has been made of it. A similar comic opera, *The Chocolate Soldier*, was based on *Arms and The Man*, first produced at Theater des Westens, Berlin, in 1909 (written by Bernauer and Jacobson, music by Oskar Straus). Shaw insisted that the programme should include an apology for 'this unauthorised parody of one of Mr. Bernard Shaw's comedies'. The librettists had, indeed, tried to get Shaw's consent for their opera, but they failed, so they took the risk and did without it. Shaw could do little as the opera was produced in Berlin. But its success seemed to win him over, and he offered no objection to the opera's first London production at the Lyric Theatre, in the September of the following year. *The Chocolate Soldier* (in whole or in part) was a very popular item at amateur performances, for example, at school concerts and other similar functions.

During 1965 the demand for Shakespearian plays abroad waned from its peak in the quatercentenary year, and firm requests for Shaw were reported by representatives of visiting English companies on the Continent. 'G.B.S. returns from "exile" in triumph' was one newspaper headline. In 1966 Shaw was again a big box office success, more than at any time since his death, and three Shaw plays were running in London at one and the same time – *Man and Superman*, *You Never Can Tell* and *The Philanderer*. Meanwhile their popularity was reflected in the appeal of Shaw in the provinces. The Shaw revival which had begun with *My Fair Lady* was now an established fact.

In his lifetime Shaw was his own publicity agent. Modesty was not one of his strong points and he always believed that it pays to advertise

In England, as elsewhere, the spontaneous recognition of really original work begins with a mere handful of people and propagates itself so slowly that it has become a commonplace to say that genius, demanding bread, is given a stone after its possessor's death. The remedy for this is sedulous advertisement. Accordingly, I have advertised myself so well that I find myself almost as legendary a person as the Flying Dutchman.

My chief contribution to my generation has been my great success (*sic*) in stimulating the thoughts of men and women. With each new play I have brought a message to mankind. Indeed, in the realm of ideas I may be called the messenger boy of my time. Viewed as a whole my work has been thoroughly constructive; each play is a testament of my convictions.

One cannot quarrel with what he says usually, the only thing is that it would sound better coming from somebody else. We dislike a sense of superiority in a man and we have a distrust of the sincerity of the man who pushes himself to the forefront and wonder if he is trying to hoodwink the public. The tone of many passages such as the one quoted makes one wonder how far they are to be taken seriously. A lot of this sort of talk was bravado. Shaw set himself up as a crank and had to live the part. That is the reason why so many contradictory things have been said about him, all of which can be substantiated from his work. Sir Oliver Lodge, for instance, declared that *Androcles and the Lion* was 'profoundly religious', while prominent ecclesiastics denounced it as thoroughly irreligious. In Arland Ussher's *Three Great Irishmen* the title of the first is 'Bernard Shaw: Emperor and Clown' – two extremes. In his seemingly most earnest moments we can never be quite sure that he is not jesting, and he likes to keep up this attitude of mystery and meanwhile he just chuckles at our bewilderment. Thus to one he is a great man of genius, while to another he is a sheer humbug. One is tempted to apply to him Shakespeare's line 'O Heavens! were man but constant he were perfect'.

Some of Shaw's friendships were bizarre for a man of letters. In 1929, when he was over seventy, he went for a holiday with Gene Tunney, the boxer, in Italy (a country at that time under the rule of one of Shaw's heroes). The only thing they seemed to have in common was that (in different ways) they both knew how to hit out. Shaw was, however, interested in prize-fighters in boyhood and in his youth had himself a reputation as a fighter of some note. After that he became a fighter in another sense and spent his life dealing blows with his pen.

And what of Shaw's future reputation in the great heritage of English Literature? In 1956 the Public Trustee Office valued his copyrights at £430,000, so that there is no doubt that considerable sales of his works were expected. Shaw himself was convinced that he would be 'a panjamdrum of literature for the next three hundred years'. That remains to be seen. Joseph Woodkrutch, the American author, has a very different view. 'It was chiefly as a stimulant that he was valuable. . . . A showman of ideas, he became the victim of his own showman's gift, and he will probably be remembered neither as a playwright nor as a philosopher, but chiefly as a man who beat a drum so effectively that he enticed an apathetic public to that main tent where greater men than he were performing.' The very fact that Shaw's plays are problem plays would indicate that when the problems of our time are no more so too will his plays be forgotten. With the possible exception of Saint Joan there are no great souled people in Shaw's plays who inspire us to carry their spirit into our own lives to make them more beautiful and worthy. His plays start with ideas and problems, not with people. His aim is the dramatisation of a problem, not complete presentation of character. His characters attract him by their relationship as members of society rather than as individuals. In this he is typical of his age.

Shaw was never tired of comparing himself with Shakespeare, and Shakespeare generally came off worse. Shakespeare was inferior because he had no message for his time. Shaw sent out his first play with the self-assurance of 'If my play *Widowers' Houses* is not better than Shakespeare, let it be damned promptly,' and one of his publicity stunts was to keep up the comparison, sometimes in not too good taste, as when he spoke about 'people like me and Shakespeare'. But to this editor it is unthinkable that Shaw will ever enjoy a comparable reputation. In the Preface to the *Three Plays for Puritans* he said that *Caesar and Cleopatra* was 'An offer to my public of my Caesar as an improvement on Shake-speare's'. Compared with Shakespeare's Caesar and Cleopatra Shaw's seem more like parodies. *Caesar and Cleopatra* is flippant by the side of the intensity of feeling in *Antony and Cleopatra*. Androcles and Ferrovius and Lavinia have not that sense of universality that informs Shakespeare's figures. Shakespeare lays bare human character, emotions that are eternal – love and hate, joy and sorrow, envy and ambition – great human qualities and little human oddities, in language that is a continual joy to every generation. Shaw's plays present his own views on the problems of his time. Shakespeare said that the stage should 'mirror nature,' but it would appear from the Prefaces that Shaw thinks that the stage should *explain* nature. Shaw said (among many other things about the drama), 'A play with a discussion is a modern play. A play with only an emotional situation is an old-fashioned one.' But Shaw's witty discussion is no substitute for Shakespeare's emotional power. His plays are intellectually keen, crushingly witty, but cynical in tone, without men and women who stir our being. Their appeal is more to the head than to the heart. Whereas Shakespeare could write of mankind, 'What a piece of work is man! how noble in reason! how infinite in faculty! in form and moving how express and admirable! in action how like an angel! in apprehension how like a god! the beauty of the world! the paragon of animals!' Shaw says, 'When I die and go to heaven I shall feel bound in intellectual honour to say to God, "Scrap the lot, Old Man. Your human experiment is a failure. Men as political animals are quite incapable of solving the problems created by the multiplication of their own numbers. Blot them out and make something better!"' With this cynical view of mankind, little wonder that he has made his mark attacking and not enjoying humanity. Wit, satire and irony abound in his plays, but genial human tolerance, no. When Shaw laughs he laughs *at* people not *with* them, and his humour leaves a sting. His sneer for his fellow creatures is repellent. He enjoys wrenching the weaknesses out of human nature more than showing its greatness. He loves to take a stand on his own – paradoxically turning everything inside out, so that what is accepted on all hands as the truth is seen in a very different light. Romantic delusions must be swept away. Whatever is accepted by the general run of mankind Shaw is bound to attack. He likes to be put on his mettle to defend an argument that is hard to defend. Apparently English people like home truths. At any rate by running them down Shaw has made a bigger impression on his day and generation than any other of his contemporaries. But, looking to the future, those artists of past ages who are still loved by humanity are those who have had a love of humanity themselves. By no stretch of the imagination can Shaw be said to have this. He examines and overhauls mankind like a garage-hand repairing a car, and then gives it up as a bad job and tells the boss that he had better 'scrap the lot'.

Shaw died on 2nd November, 1950, as the result of a fall a few months earlier. In the Preface to *Pygmalion* he says that it is his zeal for the reform of the English language that has induced him to write a play in which the hero is an 'energetic phonetic enthusiast'. The extent of his interest in the reform of English may be judged from the fact that in his will most of his large fortune (£367,233 13s.) was left for a scheme for reforming the English alphabet. (He was man of the world enough, however, to include a clause under which, if this turned out to be impracticable, the money should be divided between the National Gallery of Ireland, the British Museum and the Royal Academy of Dramatic Art.) Six years after his death Shaw's alphabet bequest was declared invalid in the Chancery Court, but on appeal the Public Trustee was allowed to carry out the direction in Shaw's will to 'employ a phonetic expert to transliterate my play entitled *Androcles and the Lion* into the proposed British Alphabet'. (Shaw chose a short play for the purpose, be it noted.) The four equal winners of a competition held with that in view, with the co-operation of Sir James Pitman produced 'The Shaw Alphabet Edition of *Androcles and the Lion*', which was published as a Penguin Book in 1962, page by page alongside the ordinary text. It takes up much less space, and, indeed, looks like a kind of shorthand.

It was hoped to raise a great National Memorial Fund in Shaw's honour, to give assistance to causes which would have appealed to him, and also to keep Shaw's Corner, his house at Ayot St. Lawrence (where he had lived since 1906), open as a National Memorial. The organising committee appealed for £250,000; they received £407, and the whole scheme had to be abandoned.

This sorry tale makes a bitter commentary on Shaw's confident boasts. Fortunately his house has since become a property of the National Trust (to whom he left it) and is open to the public daily (except Mondays). In the course of a year there are over 10,000 visitors, though whether their interest in Shaw derives from the plays or from *My Fair Lady* is open to question.

Since his death Shaw's works have been widely read, and when his plays have been produced in the theatre audiences have been well up to the average. His plays are often broadcast on the radio and shown on television. *Arms and The Man* was twice broadcast as a World Theatre production (with Sir Ralph Richardson as the Shavian and Sir John Gielgud as the traditional type of hero).

The play

Title

Arms and The Man was at first called *Alps and Balkans*, but one place is as good as another, for the play concerns human attitudes. The title which replaced it was taken from the first line of Dryden's translation of Virgil's *Aeneid* ('Arms and the man I sing'). The play was finished, said Shaw, 'before I had decided where to set the scene, and then it only wanted a word here and there to put matters straight,' adding, 'you see, I know human nature!'

The details of the scene are correct, however. All the places are actual places, and there was actually a battle of Slivnitsa, where the Serbs were defeated by the Bulgarians in 1885. It can hardly be believed today that when it was first produced there was an over-serious critic who objected to the setting of the play because it would not help the cause of liberation of the Balkans if Bulgarians were presented as a people not given to washing their hands and necks.

Plot

Raina Petkoff, only child of a wealthy Bulgarian, retires for the night after adoring the portrait of her beloved Sergius, an officer in the army of the Bulgarians, now at war with the Serbs, who has just been reported 'the hero of the hour, the idol of the regiment' in a recent battle. An officer of the pursued Serbian army climbs into Raina's bedroom and Raina hides him and abets his escape (meanwhile feeding him on chocolate creams). The fugitive gives her to understand that he is a Swiss mercenary and he shatters some of Raina's romantic ideals concerning war and the soldiers who fight it.

On a fine spring morning just over three months later the war is over and the warriors return – first Major Petkoff, Raina's father, then Sergius, her lover, and then the fugitive from Act I (Captain Bluntschli), who has come to return the disguise that he was lent in Act I. Sergius and Raina agree that they have found the 'higher love', but that does not stop Sergius from flirting with the maid. Bluntschli is invited to stay by Major Petkoff; Raina in her turn betrays a greater interest in 'the chocolate soldier' than in Sergius. He was lately come into property which makes him an acceptable suitor to the parents, and in the end Raina agrees to marry Bluntschli, while Sergius, whose nature it is never to withdraw, refuses to withdraw from marrying Louka.

The way in which the lovers are balanced against one another should be noticed.

Raina loses a pose of affection for Sergius, due to spontaneous attraction to Bluntschli.

Sergius loses a pose of affection for Raina, due to spontaneous attraction to Louka.

Meanwhile Nicola and Louka act as a foil 'below stairs' to Sergius and Raina.

The actual events are rather 'thin' and are not to be taken seriously; the real interest is in these parallel attitudes and the opposition in the character of Bluntschli.

Act summaries, critical commentary, textual notes and revision questions

Act I

The first act of the play is the most exciting.

Late in November 1885, the Serb army is in headlong retreat before the Bulgarians in the streets of a small Balkan town. Raina Petkoff, the only child of a rich Bulgarian, a major in the Bulgarian army, before she goes to bed shows adoration for the portrait of her beloved, Sergius, the hero of the hour. After she is in bed a Serb fugitive clambers up to the balcony of the house and enters her bedroom. He is hidden by Raina and, with her help, survives a search. In the course of conversation he discloses that he is a Swiss mercenary employed in the Serbian army and he dissipates some of her most cherished illusions about war and manhood. As soon as Raina has left him to go and tell her mother (Catherine) of his presence in her room, the intruder falls fast asleep in her bed, where 'the brute' is found by a shocked mother.

The setting is deliberately ironic, with contrast between poverty and wealth, taste and lack of it. In fact it is anti-romantic, with the emphasis on the fake rather than the real, on what appears rather than what is. The novels and the chocolate creams underline the idea of romance which is not derived from reality, and since this is one of the major themes of the play, the posturing of Raina before she actually speaks makes the viewer or reader understand that she too is given over to self-indulgence rather than real feeling. The wit in the description is pungently effective with regard to Catherine.

Note that the reactions of the two women are based on hearsay, and that they have willed Sergius to be 'the hero of the hour' anyway. The mother is as absurdly romantic as the daughter. Notice that the conventional worshipping of the hero is regarded as more important than anything else. But Raina has insights into herself and the romantic notions of others, and casts a refreshing area of doubt (soon to be swallowed in self-indulgent ecstasy) which anticipates what is to come, the reality of war instead of the romantic ideas. Louka makes an immediate impact. She is not the conventional servant but an independent one. The business with the shutters is practical stagecraft which emphasises the doubleness of Raina who, although she is so happy, hankers after being involved, almost inviting a fugitive before one arrives. Louka of course understands this. Stage directions as Raina mimes are significant – note the use of the word 'priestess' to define Raina's 'worship' of Sergius (or is it only the picture of Sergius?).

There is a neat play too on fiction and reality. The shooting and the entry of the fugitive are dramatic (almost as if we were not watching a comedy), but a deliberate unromantic note is struck with the description of the man. He is nondescript but individualized, facing Raina with the truth and not the fiction of: 'It is our duty to live as long as we can'. But his change of mood when he thinks he is going to be taken is effective and shows Raina another kind of reality – real not posturing chivalry. And the further ironic stroke is shown when he tells her that almost all soldiers are stupid, and is proved completely right when the search fails to uncover his obvious hiding position. Of course there is something essentially romantic in Raina's action in hiding the enemy. Dramatic effectiveness is shown in Louka seeing the revolver on the ottoman – this rouses tension in the audience and again underlines the man's point about the stupidity of the soldiers. The young Russian officer is almost a parody of the romantic conception of a soldier. Despite the shooting the situation is farcical, almost a Shavian parody of the bedroom farce so dear to the hearts of English theatregoers. With the officer's retreat Louka's 'insolence' (not at first understood by Raina) comes into its own. The anti-romantic tone continues through the revelation that the man is a mercenary, not even committed to the ideals for which each side is supposedly fighting. Chocolates not cartridges now supply the debunking ammunition. The description of the cavalry charge and its effect is deliberately diminished by the language ('like slinging a handful of peas against a window pane'). The fact that there is no ammunition again reduces the heroics to a farcical dimension, but Raina's production of the portrait is undercut by the stage direction that the man feels she might be going to get something more for him to eat. This soon gives way to laughter, but the farce continues with his reaction to the idea of climbing down the waterpipe, which seems to scare him more than actually being confronted by the enemy — or even by the idea of having to think and make decisions and exert himself. The fact that all he wants is sleep certainly makes for pathos. Shaw is always adept at the dramatic effect, and Raina's pulling the man back is just that — it is almost as if she is moving from romance to reality through the facts of the situation. This is followed by the superb comedy of cleanliness, with Raina's hands being kissed while the man keeps his obviously dirty ones behind his back. When Raina leaves his need for sleep becomes paramount, and this leads to Catherine and Raina confronting one another at the end of the scene. Already Raina is showing that she is capable of change — that she is responding to the needs of the man as a man and not as a (supposed) hero. The dramatic curtain shows that Catherine, conditioned to romantic detestation of the enemy, thinks of him as 'The brute'.

Bulgaria From 1878 Bulgaria had a troubled history, and hence it is a suitable setting for an out-of-the-way war with situations common to all wars in all places.

Dragoman Pass A mountain pass between Bulgaria and the old Serbia (now between Bulgaria and Yugo-Slavia). Slivnitza, 18 m. N.W. of Sofia, is on the way to the Dragoman Pass.

Byron and Pushkin Romantic poets (English and Russian respectively) of the early nineteenth century who died dramatic deaths which appealed to the popular imagination, one as a volunteer liberator of Greece (although his death was due to fever), the other in a duel.

act its romance Notice the double meaning of the word 'act'.

Don Quixote The 'knight of the doleful countenance' in Cervantes' romance of that name (1605), who had most absurd adventures (such as charging 'at the windmills').

a chocolate cream soldier! The title of the opera on *Arms and The Man*.

the opera of Ernani By Verdi (1844). It is based on the tragedy *Hernani*, by Victor Hugo.

Castilian Castile was (and is) a central district of Spain.

Revision questions on Act I

1 Write a character sketch of Raina as she appears in this Act. In what ways does she develop?

2 Write a short essay on Shaw's use of either irony or farce in this Act.

3 Show how the anti-romantic theme is presented here.

4 Write an essay on the parts played by Catherine and Louka

Act II

On 6th March following, a fine spring morning, in the garden of Major Petkoff's house man-servant and maid-servant discuss a servant's position in a household. It is after breakfast. The war is over and the master somewhat unexpectedly returns. Louka, the maid-servant, brings out the breakfast to which he was accustomed aforetime. His wife comes from the house, gives him a rather formal welcome, and in the course of conversation both express narrow-minded opinions. Major Saranoff (Sergius) also comes back from the war, but Catherine gives *him* a hearty welcome. He states that he is no longer a soldier and utters some anti-romantic opinions about the act of war. He then tells a 'queer story' about how a 'bagman of a captain', 'a commercial traveller in uniform', escaped by climbing a waterpipe – essentially the story of Act I. After a protest from Raina about the indelicacy of the story, Sergius apologises. Catherine engineers a tête-à-tête between Raina and Sergius, but after calling Raina 'his lady and his saint' and talking of 'pure passion', as soon as she has gone Sergius throws off the strain by flirting with the maid. Louka (the maid) lets slip a hint of the affair of the intruder and Sergius is scandalised. He then joins Major Petkoff in the library to discuss army affairs.

Thereupon a 'Captain Bluntschli' is introduced. It is the night intruder, who has brought back the Major's coat, which was lent him when he escaped. Catherine tries to get him to go quickly, by telling him a mixture of lies, but is forestalled by the arrival of her husband and Sergius, when Bluntschli is constrained to accept their hospitality for a little while.

The student should note how the characters are successively paired off in this act, the couples appearing in this rather formal and prescribed manner:

1. Louka and Nicola.
2. Catherine and Petkoff (later with Sergius and Raina, leading to)
3. Sergius and Raina.

4. Sergius and Louka.
5. Catherine and Raina.
6. Captain Bluntschli and Catherine.
7. And in the final episode all are on the stage together, with the exception of Louka (but including Nicola for a time).

The dialogue with Nicola shows Louka's independence and his cunning subservience: class differences are spelled out, and we feel that both servants are looking to the main chance. Louka comes across as a girl of potent sexuality (this anticipates her flirtation with Sergius), and Nicola as the middle-aged (nearly) subservient servant who in fact is storing up quite a bit of information about the family, doubtless to be put to use at the right time. Petkoff's arrival sparks expectation, but the emphasis is distinctly unromantic, his wish to settle into the established routine being the main idea, even down to the cognac. By comparison his wife's greeting is perfunctory to say the least. Catherine's patriotism is quickly submerged in Petkoff's languid realism about the state of the peace. There is some more neat wit about washing of the neck bringing about sore throats, Shaw, via Petkoff, indulges his own irony as to the extent of the English and their washing. The game of keeping up with one's allies is played through the library and the electric bell, and the bickering between Catherine and Paul continues through the tit-for-tat exchange over shouting for the servants and hanging out the washing. Petkoff further puts down Sergius by emphasising his incompetence – 'he could throw away whole brigades instead of regiments', but Shaw's ironic description of the Major is a complete put down – he is a poseur of the first water, self-conditioned into believing in himself. Part of Shaw's innuendo is here directed at Catherine, who 'rises effusively to greet him'. He is obviously her romantic hero, the main focus of her sentiment instead of the commonsense, down to earth and commonplace husband. There is some dramatic effect when Sergius announces his resignation, but both he and Raina are intent on posing, on setting themselves out to greatest photogenic advantage. Catherine's accusation that her daughter is always listening so that she can present herself at the right moment shows her jealousy. Notice that in these exchanges there is not one natural movement of affection. Notice the dramatic effect of the mention of 'that Swiss fellow', with each of the women responding in a questioning way which shows that they are intent on covering up. As the conversation develops, so does the dramatic irony, since the author knows what the men here don't know, that the two women who sheltered the fugitive are in fact Raina and Catherine. Notice too how the story has been embroidered in the telling. Throughout, Sergius' inherent snobbery shows itself. But Raina shows her presence of mind and duplicity, Catherine her hypocrisy in the memorable 'If such women exist, we should be spared the knowledge of them'. Another fine thrust is the cutting short of Sergius' long speech by Petkoff, and the tactful way in which Catherine leaves the lovers together. Their initial exchange on being left so is operatic. Both are now intent on playing the romantic game, of maintaining the image that each expects of the other. This is soon dissipated when Sergius admits to Louka the difficulty of keeping up the higher love. He soon demonstrates his need for the earthly one, but Louka delivers a fine and unexpected stroke when she counters his deception with a smart reference to Raina's. Yet in these exchanges at least Sergius – or the six Sergiuses – is revealed to have some self-knowledge. Louka as always acts as a marker of common sense – she forecasts that one day Raina and 'the man' will marry, since she, as a servant, clearly understands the difference between appearance and reality. When he grips her we see that she is visibly affected, but not so much that she cannot use the number 'six' herself – 'I'm worth six of her [Raina]'. She is here seeking to make herself his equal despite the fact that she is a servant. The bruise incident – the bruise is reality – and his recoil from it merely emphasises the difference between them.

Notice that Raina's hat is only last year's, another ironic description. The conversation with Catherine is filled with apprehension but is effective dramatically, since we don't know how each will react until Raina takes it upon herself to put her mother down. But it is not a needless putting down – there is a strong truth in her assertion that Catherine ought to marry Sergius, and her affected anger with the Swiss officer is no more than that. Louka's next entrance is correspondingly dramatic – she enjoys putting Catherine on the spot – and Catherine's own preparations take on a farcical speed, as when she uses the salver as a mirror. Audience anticipation is now high. The speed and movement of the actors here is important. It increases with the entrance of Petkoff and Sergius, so that the audience (and Catherine) are on tenterhooks as to what will ensue. There is superb dramatic irony in the exchange between Raina and Bluntschli. Nicola (only a servant) has to bear the brunt of the blame for bringing in Bluntschli's bag. There is a wonderful flow of dramatic irony at the end of the scene, the women being triumphant with the connivance of Bluntschli.

levas The value of the lev (the standard currency unit of Bulgaria) was something over 5p at that time.

cognac brandy (Fr.).

at Bucharest Several important treaties were signed in Bucharest during the nineteenth century.

Philippopolis The Greek name (Philip's city, *i.e.* Philip of Macedon) of the city of Plovdiv, in Southern Bulgaria.

Byronism See note p. 29. *Childe Harold's Pilgrimage* was written by Byron, purporting to describe the travels through Europe of a man who, disgusted by the life of contemporary society, seeks diversion in travel.

Cossack The name of a Turkish tribe politically subject to Russia, especially as light horse in the Russian army.

ecru of the colour of unbleached linen, a pale yellow-brown shade.

bagman A contemptuous term for a commercial traveller, who, before the days of his successor in a motor-car (called a 'representative'), carried his samples in a 'bag'. It will be seen later that he carried 'a big carpet bag'.

Pirot A town in Yugo-Slavia, a little way over the Dragoman Pass from Sofia.

Egad This seems a more harmless oath than 'By God!'

Sofia The capital of Bulgaria, not far from the Dragoman Pass.

Bring the gentleman out here at once This, of course, is a stage necessity.

Revision questions on Act II

1 Describe the parts played by Nicola and Louka in the events of this Act.

2 Give in outline, supported by quotations, the main aspects of Sergius's character as it is revealed in Act II.

3 By close reference to the text, indicate the part played by dramatic irony in this Act.

4 'The women are really the centre of interest.' How far would you agree with this estimate of *Arms and the Man* from evidence in Act II?

Act III

In the library (a poor sort of place) after lunch Bluntschli helps Petkoff and Sergius out of a difficulty (see the end of the previous scene). After the Major grumbles about the disappearance of his 'old coat' (the one returned by Bluntschli), Nicola is sent to fetch it by Catherine and he finds it in its usual place. Raina talks to Bluntschli in defence of her character – in spite of her lies striking 'the noble attitude and the thrilling voice', but Bluntschli takes the wind out of her sails. Raina now tells Bluntschli that she put her portrait in a pocket of the coat he took away, and is astounded to hear that he has not found it. However, she cleverly abstracts it – as she thinks, before her father has noticed it.

Bluntschli receives a heap of letters and telegrams – his father has died. It is a mystery what he has been left – 'If you only knew!' His apparent lack of grief gives Louka an opportunity to dispraise him to her mistress, in order to annoy her, and it is significant that this does annoy her.

Nicola makes an approach to Louka – not love – he regards a wife as an investment; but Louka tells Sergius that Raina will never marry him, 'she will marry the Swiss'. Sergius challenges the Swiss to a duel, from which he soon finds honourable reason to withdraw. Raina guesses that Louka is Sergius's informant that the 'queer story' he told at the beginning of Act II concerned Bluntschli and herself.

But the Major had seen the billet-doux from Raina to Bluntschli and upon enquiry discovers the truth. Raina declares that Sergius has changed his mind and introduces Louka as the object of Major Saranoff's affections. After his utilitarian fashion Nicola disclaims any interest in Louka. Bluntschli declares that he brought the coat back in person in order 'to have another look at the young lady', and mention of the coat reveals to Major Petkoff where it has been. Bluntschli proposes formally to become a suitor for Raina's hand, and, after some objection from her parents, shows in a satirical climax that he can make a better offer than Sergius. Raina meanwhile objects 'to be sold to the highest bidder', but Bluntschli points out how she accepted him as 'a fugitive, a beggar, and a starving man', and she succumbs 'with a shy smile'. Bluntschli suddenly becomes business-like, as at the beginning of the act, and, announcing the exact time of his return, clicks his heels, makes a military bow and goes.

A wonderful still-life ironic opening through the setting. The incongruity of the room is matched by the incongruity of the characters. Despite the gaze of Raina, romance appears to have gone out of the window. Note that Bluntschli is the practical man. Much depends on that already well-tried prop, the coat, and there is a continuing dramatic irony in Nicola being sent out to get it. Bluntschli's 'Madame is sure to be right!' carries its own resonance for the audience. There is easy, natural comedy in how the men are to be told what to do, but the real dramatic effect is seen in the fact that Raina and Bluntschli, being left alone, she is able to tell him what has happened, to bring him up to date on the events. She naively – or cunningly, tries to preserve her own romantic notions of Sergius, and the conversation about lies shows Shaw probing an essential truth – that lies are natural and that we protest too much if we think that we don't tell them. The other truth is the probing of reality in the human personality as distinct from the image that people present to the world and which they like to believe in themselves. At least Raina has the self-honesty to define the act she puts on and to share the joke with Bluntschli: she has probably never been more natural in her life. But she certainly responds to his suggestion that underneath his exterior Sergius is probably like that too – aware of his image and aware of his reality (he has already shown this with Louka). The master-stroke here is Raina's revelation that the portrait was in the coat which, as I said earlier, is the prop that very nearly takes over the action.

The dramatic tension having been thus further raised,

Raina resumes her own posturing. Bluntschli takes this easily in his stride (note his refusal to be put out until later). The pace of the drama continues to quicken, Louka's delivery of the letters arousing expectation, for we register Bluntschli's ecstatic cries: this is clue-laying on Shaw's part. Nicola's coining of money makes a neat contrast to the affectations of Raina: his account of how he has 'made' Louka again turns romance on its head in favour of economic practicalities. Nicola's implication is definitely that money comes first in all his calculations, and this is demonstrated later in the play. Here we feel, not to put too fine a point on it, that he would prefer to be Louka's pimp than her husband. Sergius' words about bravery smack rather of realism than of romance, and they ironically look forward to a relaxing of the class distinctions which characterise the play. Some of the comedy however depends on the continuation of his posturing. This soon breaks down in the face of Louka's home truths, and he is – or affects to be – tormented by jealousy. Louka ironically underlines her own romantic nature (but perhaps there is a practicality beneath it) by saying that she would dare everything and marry for love. There is some tension in Sergius promising to marry Louka, for although we may feel that this is romance we are now intrigued by the movement of the plot. Will the opportunity present itself?

Bluntschli's coolness is itself a mockery of the duel situation which develops. So calm is he – so apparently unromantic – that he is able to comfort Raina, who naturally wants to read something romantic (love for her) into their motivation. Bluntschli continues to dominate the situation, his remark about Raina not knowing whether he is married or not completely diminishing her. But Sergius also contributes his share of truth, superbly equating war and love as shams. Raina naturally melodramatises the fact that Sergius has flirted with Louka. Revelation follows quickly upon revelation, the farce of the duel fully exposed when Raina suggests that Sergius will have to fight his 'rival' Nicola for Louka's affections. Raina appears to win at every turn here but, to her credit, though she tries to rouse the romantic reactions, she cannot do so and succumbs to her own comic good sense. After the discovery of the eavesdropping Louka the coat once more becomes the focus of attention and dramatic revelation. Raina 'dexterously' manages it well, her actions provocative but underlining *her* feeling for Bluntschli. Petkoff's revelation sets everything into farcical movement again. Speed as always in the play is of the essence. Bluntschli's wonderful 'shall I ever forget their flavour!' is an anti-romantic gem. Nicola seizes his opportunity, Louka hers. But Bluntschli has the important words through his fine sense of comic opportunism (does he really think that Raina is only 17?) The *denouement* has his revelations about property and possessions: they make him paradoxically an acceptable romantic, 'chocolate cream soldier' with all the economic weight to smooth the practical and romantic way. Even to the end he is the efficient organiser in a world of romantic inefficiency. The Shavian irony plays over the happy ending.

hookah A pipe in which the smoke is drawn through water and a long flexible tube before it reaches the smoker's mouth.

levas See note p. 33.

Hand aufs Herz! My hand on my heart!

Pirot See note p. 34.

He has left ... hotels behind him *Cf.* what Sergius said in Act II, 'His father was a hotel and livery stable keeper; and he owed his first step to his knowledge of horse-dealing'.

Louka [*knowing instinctively ... Bluntschli*]. *Cf.* what Louka said to Sergius in Act II, 'And I tell you that if that gentleman ever comes here again, Miss Raina will marry him, whether he likes it or not. I know the difference between the sort of manner you and she put on before one another and the real manner'.

Klissoura Klisura (now the usual spelling) is situated about 60 m. east of Sofia.

there shall be no mistake ... this time *Cf.* Act I, 'But when the sergeant ran up as white as a sheet, and told us theyd sent us the wrong ammunition, and that we couldnt fire a round for the next ten minutes, we laughed at the other side of our mouths. I never felt so sick in my life; though Ive been in one or two very tight places. And I hadnt even a revolver cartridge.'

cried on agreed.

I have two hundred horses 'Worn out chargers', 'not even eatable', according to Major Petkoff in Act II.

I have three native languages In different parts of Switzerland, French, German and Italian are spoken.

Timok The valley of the River Timok extends from the Dragoman Pass to the Danube.

Lom Palanka A town on the Danube – the northern boundary of Bulgaria.

Is he a man? Or is he something more? – He is so efficient.

Revision questions on Act III

1 What are the main objects of Shaw's attack in this final section of the play?

2 Which character do you prefer of all those on stage in Act III? Give reasons for your choice, and quote from the play in support of what you say.

3 Indicate the part played by the coat and the portrait in Act III.

4 Write about any three incidents in this Act which demonstrate the nature of Shaw's humour. Again, quote from the play in your answer.

The characters

There is no list of characters furnished in Shaw's plays. He did not wish the actors to steal the interest of his characters in the parts they represented. These are the characters in *Arms and The Man*.

The Man (Captain Bluntschli, a captain in the Serbian army).

Raina Petkoff, a young lady of wealthy family.

Catherine Petkoff, her mother.

Major Paul Petkoff, her father.

Major Sergius Saranoff, her betrothed.

A young Russian officer in Bulgarian uniform. (In the first performance this part was taken by A. E. W. Mason, who afterwards became famous as a writer of popular adventure novels.)

Nicola, a man-servant.

Louka, Miss Raina's maid, also carrying out general household duties.

From the beginning of his career as a dramatist Shaw accepted the theatre for propaganda purposes. He took his mission seriously, and all his plays have a message. But the whole object of the stage is to show men and women living before us, laying bare what they are by the way they respond to certain situations. Characters must be men and women before they are attached to ideas. In the long run they must stand or fall by their own individuality. Shaw started with the message first. He himself acknowledged this. *Arms and The Man*, however, is not only a play with a message or a thesis. Take away the theme and it is an amusing play in its own right, and the characters have an interest in their own right too. 'If I make you laugh at yourself', said Shaw in the Preface to an edition of his plays in 1934, 'remember that my business as a classic writer of comedies is "to chasten morals with ridicule", and if I sometimes make you feel like a fool, remember that I have by the same action cured your folly, just as the dentist cures your toothache by pulling out your tooth. And I never do it without giving you plenty of laughing gas.' Human foibles are thrown into relief by comic exaggeration.

Other remarks on Shaw's presentation of his characters will be found in the section on Style. The student will notice the way that the characters stand out in sharp contrast to each other. This is even more striking on the stage.

Raina

Youve found me out.

There is no full-length portrait of Raina in *Arms and The Man*, as there is of Bluntschli and Sergius. The fullest is in the first part of Act II, beginning, 'She makes a charming picture'.

We first see Raina standing on a balcony 'intensely conscious of the romantic beauty of the night, and of the fact that her own youth and beauty are part of it'. She is a girl of romantic nature brought up in luxury, one of 'the family of the Petkoffs, the richest and best known in our country', though it would appear that it was an upstart family. Her mother has pretensions to be a Viennese lady, but Raina's room gives evidence of considerable vulgarity, despite the boast that the family was twenty years old. (Shaw's way of saying that all wealthy families are of small duration beside time in the world.) Her daughter, however, is convinced that she is a Bulgarian 'of really good standing', for does she not live in 'the only private house that has two rows of windows' and does she not wash her hands 'nearly every day', and does not her father own the only library in Bulgaria (notwith-standing his impatience with 'all this washing').

Raina worships her soldier-lover, her 'soul's hero', who, it is reported, has just won a great victory. She determines that she will never be unworthy of him. But the danger of battle is not her affair; as soon as she hears a shot she will 'blow out the candle and roll herself up in bed with her ears well covered'. But when one of the enemy becomes a man *in person*, not a man considered under the general label of enemy, and climbs into her room 'she draws herself up superbly, and looks him straight in the face', speaking to him with disdain. By then something about the situation or the soldier has appealed to her, and impulsively she agrees, 'I'll help you. I'll save you', though her betrothed lover and her father are fighting on the other side. Forced at pistol point to assist him on his entry, she voluntarily conceals him from a search, gives him what food she can and helps him to escape. In the course of her conversation with him Raina's romantic ideas of war are shattered. War is shown to be a matter of business, won by common sense and superior forces, not by pomp and circum-stance. Perhaps Raina's ideas had met with doubts in her mind before – 'It came into my head just as he was holding me in his arms and looking into my eyes, that perhaps we only had our heroic ideas because we are so fond of reading Byron and Pushkin, and because we were so delighted with the opera that season at Bucharest. Real life is so seldom like that!' (Note that Raina shows her fondness for opera a second time – that of *Ernani*.) But her mother cries shame on her doubts, and Raina again finds happiness and fulfilment 'that the world is really a glorious world for women who can see its glory and men who can act its romance!'

When her affianced lover comes home she resumes her volatile love romance with him, as he does with her, but the claims of a flesh and blood affair are stronger and she feels a more powerful attraction to the man whom she had rescued. 'Oh, I know Sergius is your pet,' she declares to her mother. 'I sometimes wish you could marry him instead of me. You would just suit him. You would pet him, and mother him to perfection.' She admits to a temptation to shock him and she has got to the point where she does not care 'whether he finds out about the chocolate cream soldier or not. I half hope he may.' It is clear that Sergius now takes second place in her affection. It is clear that, notwithstanding her pride in loving a national hero, ultimately political considerations play no part in her love. When Sergius is out of sight she shows 'a perceptible relaxation of manner'. Notice that this is *before* Bluntschli has come back. Louka knew by instinct the difference between genuine and affected love, 'the difference between the sort of manner you and she put on before one another and the real manner', as she told Sergius. She knows instinctively 'that she can annoy Raina by disparaging Bluntschli'. It should be noticed, however, that Sergius is the first to show signs of wanting to withdraw from their love pledge (although he never withdraws!) – by his flirting with Louka, which is natural and spontaneous, in no way a pose. Raina is a hypocrite and, when she is offended by Sergius's relating the 'queer story' involving her and Bluntschli, she rebukes him for quite another reason – his coarseness, pretending to be over-refined, whereupon Sergius apologises for his abominable behaviour. And Catherine amply supports her daughter's protest. Raina is no unworldly Tennysonian lover – indeed, she listens round the corner so as to time her appearances for the greatest effect.

When Bluntschli treats her without heroics, it is such a refreshing change to be found out and taken seriously for what she is that, after an apparent protest, she capitulates and admits to being found out. Bluntschli knows that she tells lies (in spite of her 'noble attitude' and 'thrilling voice'). So do we. Early in the play she tells the Russian officer that she has not been to bed; in the last act she helps her father on with his coat only to pick his pocket. Indeed, her whole life has been a pose from childhood. Bluntschli brings her to a denial of this as a matter of course, but after sudden realisation of it she admits that it is true and seems rather pleased and relieved by the discovery. Her love life is included in the pose. Her ideas of love are shattered by Bluntschli as her ideas of war were shattered by him on their first meeting, and with them so have her ideas of herself been shattered. It is natural that she should want to marry Bluntschli, the man who understands her better than anyone.

Thus the stock stage heroine who takes herself so seriously is made to step down from the pedestal which she has erected for herself on such flimsy foundations. The make-believe of life is stripped of first war and then love and then herself. The study of Raina is a study of the disillusionment of a sentimental and romantic girl. Shaw values realism, not idealism, which, as we have seen, he considers 'only a flattering name for romance'.

Sergius

The world is not such an innocent place as we used to think.

The description of Sergius is early in Act II, immediately after Nicola has announced him.

At first Sergius seems the Kipling type of stock stage hero, answering to Raina's preconceived idea of such – 'a regular handsome fellow, with flashing eyes and lovely moustache', though the moustache that Bluntschli gives him is not mentioned in Shaw's description. Sergius takes himself seriously and, like Raina, is made to step down from the pedestal which he has erected for himself on flimsy foundations. The self-important soldier who airs his dignity is made laughable to others. Catherine thinks that he looks 'superb' and speaks of his 'magnificent cavalry charge', but Bluntschli considers that he has simply had marvellously good luck, and Petkoff rates his chances of promotion as nil. Raina thinks that in the war he has proved himself 'worthy of any woman in the world', and Sergius does not dispute with his lady that theirs is the 'higher' love, though the 'hero of Slivnitza' and 'the apostle of the higher love' is quite content to experiment with a lower love. He calls Louka 'an abominable little clod of common clay, with the soul of a servant', but Louka has found out that 'whatever clay I'm made of, youre made of the same'. (Such a bold declaration from a servant girl would sound more startling in 1894 than it would now.) With all Sergius's romanticism, he sets common sense above the 'higher' love.

Louka. Then stand back where we cant be seen. Have you no common sense.
Sergius. Ah! thats reasonable.

And he has good sense and honesty enough to realise that he cannot swear on the honour of a gentleman. It does not need anyone as shrewd as Louka to see that if he is not 'so particular' and makes love to her behind Miss Raina's back he can care for Miss Raina but little. Sergius falls back on a formality of behaviour – 'Louka, you will please remember that a gentleman does not discuss the conduct of the lady he is engaged to with her maid.' Louka can penetrate below the formality to the heart. When Raina senses that something is wrong and (in fun, she says) guesses what it is, like her he tells lies, denying that he has been flirting with Louka – 'How can you think such a thing?'

Sergius is a sham lover as he is a sham hero. 'Oh, war! war! the dream of patriots and heroes! A fraud, Bluntschli. A hollow sham, like love.' He is mocked by the difference between what he would be and what he is. 'Mockery! mockery everywhere! everything I think is mocked by everything I do.' Like Raina, he learns by bitter experience that romance is 'a hollow sham'. He gives himself lordly airs and mistakes obstinacy and self-will for firmness. He never withdraws, is never sorry, never apologises and is bound by nothing. He just lives for himself and wants his own way. 'If I choose to love you, I dare marry you, in spite of all Bulgaria.' He will not be crossed. Louka informs him that she will not wait long, whereupon, taking a dramatic stance ('folding his arms and standing motionless in the middle of the room'), he petulantly avers that she shall wait his pleasure. Though victor over an enemy in battle (with, it would appear, a measure of good luck) he has not conquered himself. Indeed, it is he who leads Louka to remark that 'men never seem to grow up'. The critic H. C. Duffin dubbed him a 'feather-brained fool'.

Bluntschli

I cant make you see it from the professional point of view.

The description of Bluntschli is in Act I, immediately after the flame of a match is seen in the middle of the room.

There comes through the window a professional soldier, fighting only when he has to and very glad to get out of it when he has not. Like Falstaff, who carried a bottle of sack in his holster, Bluntschli finds chocolate more use than cartridges. 'You can always tell an old soldier by the inside of his holsters and cartridge boxes. The young ones carry pistols and cartridges: the old ones, grub.' He admits that his nerves go to pieces after two days under fire. The dangers he meets, however, are all part of the day's work, and he faces them in that spirit – like a workman who is sensible enough to obey safety regulations. Bluntschli faces things as they are and takes appropriate counter measures according to his common sense, whether they are in the rule-book or not. He is in the Serbian and not the Bulgarian army simply because he came across it first on his way from Switzerland. He has something in common with Sergius, however, who won the battle in 'the wrong way' while two colonels 'had their regiments routed on the most correct principles of scientific warfare' and 'two major-generals got killed strictly according to military etiquette'. Bluntschli is not a traditional officer-class soldier, he is 'like a commercial traveller in uniform. Bourgeois to his boots!' Raina tells him that he has 'a low shopkeeping mind' and thinks 'things that would never come into a gentleman's head'. He is a realist and knows that battles are won by strength and tactics. In the structure of the play he is a contrast to Sergius and to Raina, that is at the start, for both Sergius and Raina alter their ideas as the play proceeds, Raina largely as a result of his influence. When Bluntschli criticises Sergius as an amateur who thinks that fighting is an amusement, he reveals his own character, and there is some truth in Sergius's cross criticism that Bluntschli is a machine. Having just obtained the promise of a beautiful and desirable lady for his wife (on the day when he has heard of his father's death) he does not pause to consider, he suddenly finds that his time is up, appoints the day and hour of his return, clicks his heels and is gone to his father's funeral as to a business appointment. 'What a man! Is he a man?' is the final comment of the play (by Sergius).

Bluntschli's ménage for marriage, besides being a skit on marriage settlements in society generally, what

George Eliot calls 'the petty peremptoriness of the world's habits', has a particular interest too. It is said that his declaration of his means when his 'position' was challenged by the parents of his intended bride arose from the proposal of an Austrian hotel proprietor for the hand of a member of the Shaw family.

Shaw is a narrow interpreter of the 'sphere of humanity', to borrow a phrase of Ben Jonson's. He seizes on one aspect of our common human nature and gives situations in which it is shown, or rather satirised, so that his characters are more like propositions than real men and women of many varied (and often conflicting) inclinations, as men and women really are. Shaw is a didactic writer and the action is secondary to the ideas.

Minor characters

Major and Catherine Petkoff

The description of Catherine is at the end of the stage direction immediately before the play starts, and of Major Paul early in Act II, after he is heard identified only as a 'male voice outside'.

Major and Catherine Petkoff are stock types of the older generation – the conservative husband and the mother anxious for a good match for her daughter. The Major is impatient with change – what was good enough for his father is good enough for him. 'Look at my father! he never had a bath in his life; and he lived to be ninety-eight, the healthiest man in Bulgaria.' Nevertheless, he will go *some* way to meet 'these modern customs' – 'I dont mind a good wash once a week' – to keep up his position, not because he sees any need for it. But he does not believe 'in going too far' and becoming an extremist, like his wife who washes her neck every day. What he is not used to must be wrong. In spite of the latest in bells he would just as soon shout for the servants, but he is able to give his wife one piece of news concerning polite home-management – 'Civilized people dont hang out their washing to dry where visitors can see it'. The Major and his wife already know that it is a mark of extreme good taste to have a library (whether one reads the books in it or not) and Catherine is the prouder of it because it has an electric bell in it.

Whereas the Major can see Sergius's unfitness for promotion dispassionately, Catherine loses no opportunity of presenting him to her daughter as a desirable husband. 'And you! you kept Sergius waiting a year before you would be betrothed to him. Oh, if you have a drop of Bulgarian blood in your veins, you will worship him when he comes back.' When he does come back she gives him a fulsome welcome that has a purpose behind it. The Bulgarian blood of neither Raina nor Sergius is of any account, however, when a fighter for the Serbians has the means to set up a better establishment for Raina. Catherine's casuistry about Bluntschli's war-time visit is equalled only by that of her daughter.

It would appear from Raina's room that Catherine has little taste. The décor is an indiscriminate mixture of the good and the vulgar. She is *determined* to be a Viennese lady, implying that she is not naturally a lady. She has to be informed of what is good taste; she does not sense it. She judges by rule of thumb. The miscellaneous assembly of furniture and her dress ('a fashionable tea gown on all occasions') give away her origin and her pretensions. She has the money to buy expensive clothes, but no taste in dressing for different occasions. The criticism of the furniture, of course, assumes that as mistress of the house she is responsible for it and that Raina has not been allowed a free hand in the decoration of her own room. Except in enlightened households this would be the usual arrangement in those days, and, indeed, this impression seems to be Shaw's intention in the first stage direction.

Catherine's views of contemporary affairs are entirely superficial, following the official 'image', as she talks glibly of 'our gallant splendid Bulgarians' and 'the wretched Serbs', the attitude of the late Victorian music-hall, an attitude which the people of great nations were to adopt within twenty years of *Arms and The Man*.

Louka and Nicola

The description of Louka is on her first appearance early in Act I.

She likes to be in the avant-garde of fashion and is sophisticated enough to smoke in 1894. She fails to see why, if her mistress calls her Louka, she should not call her mistress Raina. Her pride is often referred to, indeed she feels worth six of her mistress. Emotionally she is nearer to the romantic outlook of Raina than the cynical outlook of Nicola, but, as a woman, she can intuitively tell when Raina really loves a man and when she is engaged as a formality, because it is 'the done thing'. She is impatient of reason and 'must behave in her own way'. Like her mistress she listens outside the door. All is fair, it is said, in love and war. In war Bluntschli listened once outside a tent – 'It's all a question of the degree of provocation. My life was at stake', and Louka is an eavesdropper when her love is at stake, and she is not ashamed.

Nicola's penetrating mind can supply plain, cynical reasons for making the best of things as they are and turning them to his own advantage. Materialism is commonly presented as a vice of the rich, but here it is seen as an attitude of mind – common to rich and poor.

NICOLA Well, you take my advice and be respectful; and make the mistress feel that no matter what you know or dont know, she can depend on you to hold your tongue and serve the family faithfully. Thats what they like; and *thats how youll make most out of them.*

LOUKA [*with searching scorn*] You have the soul of a servant, Nicola

NICOLA [*complacently*] Yes: thats the secret of success in service.

Nicola (described in the second paragraph of the stage direction to Act II) is a mercenary in much the same spirit as Bluntschli. 'Youll never put the soul of a servant into me' declares Louka, and she will marry Sergius. In his 'cold-blooded wisdom' Nicola denies his betrothal to Louka in the hope of getting her custom in the shop he intends to open – he gives up his love for possible pieces of silver some time in the future. Nicola's attitude to romance is that he would prefer Louka as one of his grandest customers, 'instead of only being my wife and costing me money'. 'I believe you would rather be my servant than my husband', replies Louka. 'You would make more out of me. Oh, I know that soul of yours.' But Nicola tells her never to mind his soul, but to listen to his advice. And his advice is that 'the way to get on as a lady is the same as the way to get on as a servant: youve got to know your place: thats the secret of it'.

Louka and Nicola are, of course, like the other characters, exaggerated satiric portraits.

Theme

In 1894, says Shaw, in the Preface to *Plays Pleasant* (p. *7/1*), 'I, having nothing but unpleasant plays in my desk [*Widowers' Houses, The Philanderer, Mrs. Warren's Profession*], hastily completed a first attempt at a pleasant one, and called it Arms and The Man.' (The other three were *Candida, The Man of Destiny, You Never Can Tell*.) Incidentally the pleasant plays proved commercially almost as unsuccessful as the unpleasant plays. Shaw goes on to say that his play is an onslaught on idealism and adds that idealism is only a flattering name for romance.

The theme of this first pleasant play, an 'anti-romantic comedy', is that common romantic impressions are delusive. Idealism is a betrayal and things should be seen as they are. Shaw is never happy unless he is denouncing accepted assumptions. The stock heroic stage soldier, he says, just does not exist out of fiction: the real soldier fights for a living, not courting a glamorous death in public view on the barricades. 'I'm a professional soldier: I fight when I have to, and am very glad to get out of it when I havnt to.' Bluntschli is efficient and can soon arrange horse forage when Major Petkoff and Sergius 'dont in the least know how to do it'. 'Youre only an amateur', he says to Sergius, 'you think fighting's an amusement.' But even Sergius (after experience of war, when he is no longer a soldier) declares that 'Soldiering, my dear madam, is the coward's art of attacking mercilessly when you are strong, and keeping out of harm's way when you are weak. That is the whole secret of successful fighting. Get your enemy at a disadvantage; and never, on any account, fight him on equal terms.' Ironically enough, the better soldier is on the losing side.

'Oh war! war!' he says in another place, 'the dream of patriots and heroes! A fraud, Bluntschli. A hollow sham, *like love.*' And the unromantic Bluntschli is the winner in the battle of love. The realistic soldier is a realist in love too: his sensible matter-of-fact approach forces the romantic lady who holds forth about the 'higher love' to show that she is just as susceptible to normal manliness (even to a man without the 'magnetism' of the 'higher love'). A romantic girl imagines that an officer's uniform cannot cover any but a chivalrous heart, but when she comes to herself she discovers that her heart goes out to a very ordinary officer who likes chocolate and does not like being the recipient of a bullet. Sergius thinks that he is a man 'of heart, blood and honor', but he 'finds himself out' and 'life's a farce'. He too becomes a very ordinary man stripped of his uniform and his pretensions – his fate is to marry Louka.

King Edward VII (then Prince of Wales), a representative of the establishment brought up in the Kipling concept of Empire, was manifestly offended at the play's satire on the soldiers of the Queen, and walked out of the theatre declaring, 'The fellow is a damned crank!' The press release said that 'His Royal Highness regretted that the play should have shown so disrespectful an attitude toward the Army'. The Prince of Wales, no doubt, enjoyed *The Charge of the Light Brigade*. Incidentally, of the actual charge, forty years before *Arms and The Man*, the French Marshal Bosquet said, 'C'est magnifique, mais ce n'est pas la guerre' (It is magnificent, but it is not war). Twenty-five years after *Arms and The Man*, at the end of the First World War, the play was immensely popular with ex-Servicemen, who knew the facts and were able to laugh at the heroics cherished behind the official façade of the War Office. In the Second World War colonels and captains and knights-at-arms were 'debunked' more fearlessly.

The regular stage soldier of the later nineteenth century was always gallant, out-numbered by the enemy, but winning through glory to victory in a righteous cause for his illustrious Queen, like Chevalier Bayard, 'le chevalier sans peur at sans reproche' (the fearless and blameless knight). He never felt tired or hungry or got dirty or had a button come off. Bernard Shaw believes that the playwright should be 'something more than a skilled liar', and that he should sweep away this sort of humbug. Or as Sergius says, 'Mockery! mockery everywhere! everything I think is mocked by everything I do. Coward! liar! fool!' In *Arms and The Man* people find out the truth, including the truth about themselves. 'I am quite aware', says Shaw in the Preface, 'that the much criticized Swiss officer in *Arms and The Man* is not a conventional stage soldier.' And later, 'Idealism, which is only a flattering name for romance in politics and morals, is as obnoxious to me as romance in ethics or religion.' Shaw rightly declares that 'every drama must present a conflict'. In *Arms and The Man* men (and women) represent ideas; the conflict in the play is the conflict between romance and reality.

While paying tribute to Shaw's far-seeing eye, going to the root of human conventions, one must admit that he has a belittling view of human heroism. Says St. John Ervine, 'Shaw never appreciated the value of full-blown valour, nor understood its heartening effect on dispirited men'. The worst in human nature attracts his notice more than the best.

Shaw's view that the power of his presentation of the ideas in his plays would influence public opinion (a public opinion that left the theatre half-empty when *Arms and The Man* was first produced) can be estimated from his remark to Sidney and Beatrice Webb that his ridicule would abolish war from the face of the earth! The irony of this after two major wars in the first half of the twentieth century (besides a smaller war – the Boer War – in a mere five years after his statement) in turn makes Shaw himself look ridiculous.

Style

Arms and The Man has a strong element of farce and must not be taken too seriously. It is quite in keeping with Shaw's ironic intention that his farce should show a serious purpose, however. There is occasionally in Shaw's plays a beauty and power of language which inspires an audience, when a deep hush descends on the theatre, in *Saint Joan*, for instance, but there is little scope for beautiful language in *Arms and The Man*, and, indeed, it would be incongruous side by side with the ridicule and mocking fun of the play. We find clever dialogue and situation rather than dramatic power. Shaw always has a keen eye for comic touches, especially when they have a sarcastic bent.

Commenting on Shaw's title *Three Plays for Puritans*, G. K. Chesterton said that 'In his work Shaw is as ugly as a Puritan'. There is, in general, little sense of grace, form and choice in Shaw's style. Like many modern authors he is not concerned with techniques of style, and he does not yearn after fine writing. The dialogue is matter-of-fact and lively. On the whole the sentences are short. His style has an intellectual quality of the first order: it is a model of clarity. But it lacks beauty: it is clear but cold. It was the matter rather than the manner of Shaw's plays that took the attention of thinking people in the nineties.

The Americanised spelling of the play (*e.g.* good-humor, clamor, neighbors) and the omission of the apostrophe (*e.g.* cant, didnt, hadnt, thats, youll) are just arbitrary tricks of style and do not affect its texture. Shaw's use is irregular, however, and although we read 'thats' and 'youre' we also find 'it's' (by the side of which 'youll' seems strange), 'I'm', 'I'll', 'Who's', 'we'd' and 'he'd' in one place and 'youd' in another. 'The war's over' with ' for the omission of a letter, as well as the possessive 's, *e.g.* 'my daughter's life'; 'madam's orders', 'Miss Raina's maid', is normal practice. Shaw had his own ideas on the representation of English sounds and being a famous author whose work was in demand he could indulge them (*e.g.* arnt). And on the representation of emphasis also. Shaw calmly dispenses with italics or inverted commas for titles, as in the Preface to *Plays Pleasant*. It is typical of his arrogance that he should presume arbitrarily to alter the conventions of a language that has developed over the centuries into a full instrument of expression of its own accord and without decree.

'The secret of Shaw's triumph', J. L. Garvin once said in *The Observer*, 'is the power of his stagecraft'. Shaw wrote with his eye on his stage. He saw every detail in the scenery and properties and left nothing to chance. In Act I 'Above the head of the bed, which stands against a little wall *cutting off the left hand corner of the room*, is a painted wooden shrine, *blue and gold*, with an *ivory* image of Christ, and a light hanging before it in a pierced metal ball suspended by *three* chains.' So the first page of the play sets out the details of a full stage even to the variegated native cloth on the chest of drawers. The stage direction to Act III is similar. Thus Shaw's scenes of 1894 are very different from the simple stage settings of modern plays.

Shaw has the power of seeing his play in detail and he makes good use of stage effects as a background. The contrast between light and darkness lends excitement to the entry of Bluntschli into Raina's bedroom – 'Nothing being visible but the glimmer of the light in the pierced ball before the image, and the starlight seen through the slits at the top of the shutters ... For an instant the rectangle of snowy starlight flashes out with the figure of a man silhouetted in black upon it. The shutters close immediately; and the room is dark again.' A match is struck and is out instantly. 'Another moment of silence and darkness . . . Then she lights a candle.'

Similarly Shaw visualises all his dramatic personae in detail and describes them at length, with the exception of Raina. These extended directions are a normal part of the play, *e.g.* 'She draws herself up superbly, and looks him straight in the face, adding, with cutting emphasis' . . . 'Sergius leads Raina forward with splendid gallantry. When they arrive at the table, she turns to him with a bend of the head: he bows; and thus they separate, he coming to his place, and she going behind her father's chair'. Sometimes the actions of the characters are described in unnecessary and trivial detail, *e.g.* 'She rolls up her *left* sleeve; clasps her arm *with the thumb and fingers of her right hand*'. Shaw was not going to allow scope for actors with initiative (or even for left-handed actors!). There are touches of detail in the properties which most dramatists would consider superfluous, for example, that a rider knocks on the door *with a whip handle*, and this *when the rider is off stage*.

The student will notice that in Act I Bluntschli is first referred to as The Voice, then, when he is seen and 'the mystery is at an end', as The Man, and only after he has been introduced by name (at the end of Act II) as Bluntschli. This is dramatic. When a character first appears, he has no claim to the interest of the audience, he has to make it. Just as the other characters of the play have to find out his name so does the reader (the spectator in the theatre has a programme, of course). This is more natural and helps to make the reader identify himself with the characters in the play.

In addition to a description of the appearance of his dramatis personae Shaw not infrequently sketches their character as well. Catherine is 'imperiously energetic',

Louka is 'a handsome proud girl ... so defiant that her servility to Raina is almost insolent', Major Petkoff 'is a cheerful, excitable, insignificant, unpolished man of about 50, naturally unambitious except as to his income and his importance in local society, but just now greatly pleased with the military rank which the war has thrust on him as a man of consequence in his town.' By doing this the dramatist dictates what we should think about his characters before we see them in action or hear their words. Half the joy of seeing (or reading) a play is to speculate on the characters and to see what life means to them from their words, actions and influence in the play. The dramatist who provides us with his official version of their characters takes away that pleasure and, incidentally, makes his work less dramatic. The play thus gives the impression of being half play and half novel, much like the dramatisations of novels done for the radio. This may help the reader (though it is doubtful), but is certainly superfluous in a stage production. It is a further indication of how Shaw wrote his plays to be read as much as to be acted.

The wit, humour and irony which are the essence of Shaw's writing need no illustration. The student will find them everywhere. Such never-to-be-forgotten repartee as

LOUKA [*with searching scorn*] You have the soul of a servant, Nicola.
NICOLA [*complacently*] Yes: thats the secret of success in service.

or such wit (Shaw's – the speaker is unconscious of it) as 'Our cavalry will be after them; and our people will be ready for them, you may be sure, *now theyre running away*'.

General questions and sample answer in note form

1 *Arms and The Man* bears the sub-title *An Anti-Romantic Comedy*. Can you justify this sub-title?
2 How far in *Arms and The Man* do you consider Shaw a propagandist rather than a dramatist?
3 Give an account in some detail of Raina's first meeting with Bluntschli (The Man).
4 Write an account of Act II, dividing it into its constituent parts.
5 'Every drama must present a conflict' (Preface). Analyse the conflict in *Arms and The Man*.
6 In the Preface Shaw says that idealism ('which is only a flattering name for romance') is obnoxious to him. Illustrate this from *Arms and The Man*.
7 'I suppose, now youve found me out, you despise me.' Explain why Bluntschli did not despise Raina.
8 'Youre only an amateur: you think fighting's an amusement' (Bluntschli to Sergius). 'Youve no magnetism: youre not a man: youre a machine' (Sergius to Bluntschli). Contrast the characters of Sergius and Bluntschli, showing how far both these statements are true.
9 To what extent is (*a*) Bluntschli, (*b*) Sergius shown to the audience in a ridiculous light? Do you regard them as characters or as caricatures?
10 'Nicola and Louka act as a foil . . . to Raina and Sergius' (p. 20). Explain how.
11 Show how the main characters of *Arms and The Man* are types of different beliefs or attitudes.
12 'Characterisation is not Shaw's strong point.' How far do you agree with this statement in the light of *Arms and The Man*?

13 Give examples from *Arms and The Man* of incidents or characters where Shaw emphasises sharp contrasts.

14 Write a short essay on Shaw's English style.

15 From *Arms and The Man* illustrate the way in which Shaw clearly sees his stage in his mind's eye.

Suggested notes for essay answer to question 1

(a) *Introduction* – general statement re romantic conceptions – far from the truth – ideal rather than real – sentiment rather than emotion – posturing rather than sincerity – living in a world of fantasy – presenting an image rather than a reality.

(b) Refer to the title with its punning suggestion by Shaw – the ridiculous posturing of Raina and Catherine – the false idealism/patriotism of the war – the entrance of Bluntschli – his account of chance, stupidity, larger than life posing – then his own needs – sleep and chocolate. His realism on war.

(c) The movement of the plot which uncovers reality – false love – posturing – acting up to image – then reality (Sergius turning straight to Louka) (practicality, sensuality, as distinct from romantic love) – Raina's duplicity too – the superficial exposed – the real gradually revealed.

(d) The classes – master/servant situation exposed – lack of real loyalty – exploitation – money – old status undermined by emergence of real feelings (and real money) – affectation exposed – romantic ideas of difference exposed – farce of coat and portrait contribute to ridiculousness of romance.

(e) *Conclusion* – Shaw as realist re human nature – evidence provided by characters and their actions, self-deceptions and duplicity – their final acceptance of change and what is below the surface – the measure of the anti-romantic plot.

Further reading

Further plays by Shaw, and particularly:

Major Barbara
Mrs Warren's Profession
Candida
Man and Superman
Caesar and Cleopatra
Pygmalion

Brodie's Notes

TITLES IN THE SERIES

Jane Austen	**Pride and Prejudice**
Robert Bolt	**A Man for All Seasons**
Emily Brontë	**Wuthering Heights**
Charlotte Brontë	**Jane Eyre**
Geoffrey Chaucer	**Prologue to the Canterbury Tales**
Geoffrey Chaucer	**The Nun's Priest's Tale**
Geoffrey Chaucer	**The Wife of Bath's Tale**
Geoffrey Chaucer	**The Pardoner's Prologue and Tale**
Charles Dickens	**Great Expectations**
Gerald Durrell	**My Family and Other Animals**
T. S. Eliot	**Selected Poems**
George Eliot	**Silas Marner**
F. Scott Fitzgerald	**The Great Gatsby** and **Tender is the Night**
E. M. Forster	**A Passage to India**
John Fowles	**The French Lieutenant's Woman**
Anne Frank	**The Diary of Anne Frank**
William Golding	**Lord of the Flies**
Graham Handley (ed)	**The Metaphysical Poets: John Donne to Henry Vaughan**
Thomas Hardy	**Far From the Madding Crowd**
Thomas Hardy	**Tess of the D'Urbervilles**
Thomas Hardy	**The Mayor of Casterbridge**
Aldous Huxley	**Brave New World**
John Keats	**Selected Poems and Letters of John Keats**
Philip Larkin	**Selected Poems of Philip Larkin**
D. H. Lawrence	**Sons and Lovers**
Laurie Lee	**Cider with Rosie**
Harper Lee	**To Kill a Mockingbird**
Arthur Miller	**The Crucible**
Athur Miller	**Death of a Salesman**
George Orwell	**1984**
George Orwell	**Animal Farm**
J. B. Priestley	**An Inspector Calls**
J. D. Salinger	**The Catcher in the Rye**
William Shakespeare	**The Merchant of Venice**
William Shakespeare	**King Lear**
William Shakespeare	**A Midsummer Night's Dream**
William Shakespeare	**Twelfth Night**
William Shakespeare	**Hamlet**
William Shakespeare	**As You Like It**
William Shakespeare	**Romeo and Juliet**
William Shakespeare	**Julius Caesar**
William Shakespeare	**Macbeth**
William Shakespeare	**Antony and Cleopatra**
William Shakespeare	**Othello**
William Shakespeare	**The Tempest**

George Bernard Shaw	**Pygmalion**
Alan Sillitoe	**Selected Fiction**
John Steinbeck	**Of Mice and Men** and **The Pearl**
Alice Walker	**The Color Purple**

ENGLISH COURSEWORK BOOKS

Terri Apter	**Women and Society**
Kevin Dowling	**Drama and Poetry**
Philip Gooden	**Conflict**
Philip Gooden	**Science Fiction**
Margaret K. Gray	**Modern Drama**
Graham Handley	**Modern Poetry**
Graham Handley	**Prose**
Graham Handley	**Childhood and Adolescence**
R. J. Sims	**The Short Story**